The Kids who Travel The World

Thunder Bay

For my parents,
Patsy and John,

Thanks for making Thunder
Bay a great place to grow up
and call home.

CANADIAN EXPAT MOM

The Kids Who Travel The World
-Thunder bay-
Written by: Lisa Stadnyk Webb
Illustrated by: Lourd Jim Diazon
Designed by: Sarah Arnold Darrigrand
www.canadianexpatmom.com
ISBN 978-602-73335-3-6
Text and Illustrations Copyright © 2016 Lisa Webb
Published by Canadian Expat Mom

The Kids who Travel The WORLD

Thunder Bay

Written by : Lisa Stadnyk Webb

Illustrated by : Lourd Jim Diazon

Designed by : Sarah Arnold Darrigrand

CANADIAN EXPAT MOM

Océane and Elodie were so excited
to be in Thunder Bay, Ontario.

This Northwestern Ontario city is special
to these sisters because that's where their
Mom grew up.

The girls couldn't wait to stay at their Grammie and Grampa's house while they visited.

Grammie knew the girls would be hungry after their plane ride, so she took them straight to the *Hoito Restaurant* for pancakes.

After everyone's bellies were full, the girls hopped onto the big scale at the front door to see how much they weighed. Their mom said she always did that when she was a little girl too.

Océane and Elodie wanted to play, so the family stopped at *Hillcrest Park*. They laughed as they chased each other around the big bell.

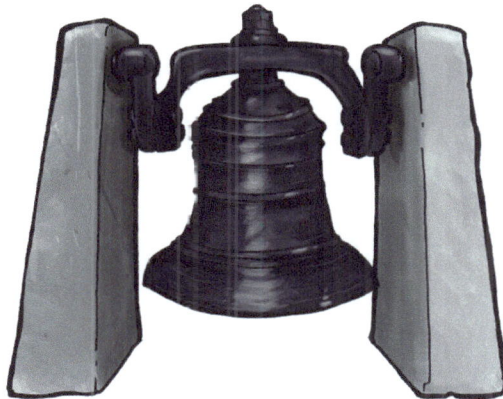

Hillcrest Park also had the best view of the *Sleeping Giant*. Legend says Nanabijou was guarding Silver Islet when he fell asleep with his hands folded over his chest.

"Let's pretend to be the Sleeping Giant!"

Océane said as she lay down with her arms folded across her chest.

Back at their grandparents' house the girls saw that Grammie had a list of things to do with the girls while they were in Thunder Bay.
They were going to be busy!

"We've already seen the Sleeping Giant!" Elodie announced happily when she saw the list.

"And we ate pancakes at the Hoito!" Océane reminded her.

See the Sleeping Giant ☑

Visit the Terry Fox monument ☐

Swim in Lake Superior ☐

Have pancakes at the Hoito ☐

Eat persians ☐

Drive to the top of Mount McKay ☐

The next day the whole family was going to camp. They packed a cooler full of yummy treats and piled into the van. Grampa said they had somewhere special to stop along the way.

The van pulled off the highway and the family got out at the *Terry Fox Monument.*

Terry Fox is a Canadian hero who wanted to run across Canada, even though he only had one leg. His journey ended in Thunder Bay and the monument is a tribute to his courage. The girls thought that he must have been very brave, and they were glad Thunder Bay had this big statue in his honour.

When they arrived at camp they saw all their cousins swimming. The sisters quickly put on their bathing suits and jumped into the lake.

Lake Superior is the biggest fresh water lake in the world and, because of its size, the water can be very cold. But the girls were too excited to notice the chilly water.

That night at camp all the family gathered around the fire and made s'mores with graham crackers, chocolate and marshmallows.
They were so yummy!

Everyone around the fire was laughing and telling stories. The girls sang songs with their cousins.
It was so much fun being at camp!

As they drove back into the city they had a look at the list their Grammie made.

Many things had been checked off, but they still had a few more activities to do while they were in Thunder Bay.

In the morning they went on another drive, but this time they drove to *Mount McKay*. They were able to drive to the top where they could see all of Thunder Bay from the lookout. Océane even spotted their Grammie and Grampa's house.

*A*fter a quick stop for
ice cream, the family took
in the sights at *Kakabeka Falls*.

Back at Grammie and Grampa's house that night they looked at the list on the fridge.
Tomorrow they would be flying home and they still hadn't tasted a persian. They wondered what a persian even was?

"It's time to go to the airport!"
their Mom announced the next morning.

"The girls can't leave just yet"
Grammie said.

She opened a box and, much to the girls'
delight, it was full of yummy pastries that
looked almost like cinnamon buns covered
with pink icing. These were persians, and
they tasted as good as they looked!

The girls felt lucky that their Mom was from Thunder Bay, because that meant they'd always come back to visit. And this was definitely a place they wanted to visit again!

CANADA

ONTARIO

Thunder Bay

Océane (pronounced oh-say-an) and Elodie are French names. These two sisters are Canadian, but they were both born in France, where their family lived for 5 years. After France, they spent a year living in Indonesia, and are now on their way to a new adventure, living in Congo.

These global girls speak English with their "**Mom**" and French with their "**Papa**". Océane and Elodie have been travelling the world together since they were born. They always look forward to exploring different places and learning new things.

*T*his book is part of a series!
Join the sisters on their exciting trips to Paris and Rome. Have your passport ready because you never know where they'll go next.

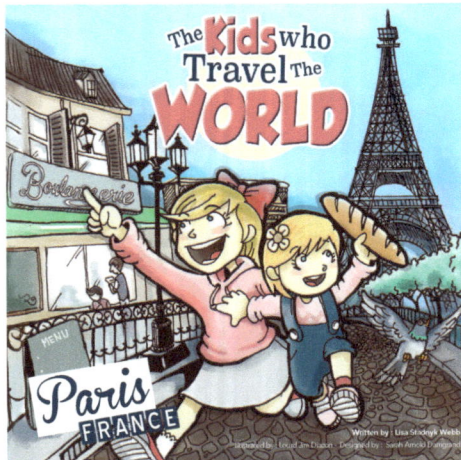

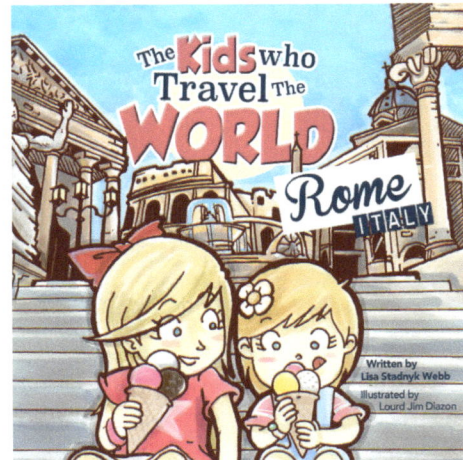

www.ingramcontent.com/pod-product-compliance
Lightning Source LLC
Chambersburg PA
CBHW042116040426
42449CB00002B/64